JEAN TURNER-ZIMMERMANN, M. D.

CHICAGO'S
BLACK TRAFFIC
— IN —
WHITE GIRLS

By

MRS. JEAN TURNER-ZIMMERMANN, M. D.

President of the

CHICAGO RESCUE MISSION and WOMAN'S SHELTER

———— AND ————

Superintendent of

The DEPARTMENT OF PURITY AND HEREDITY of the COOK COUNTY W. C. T. U.

733 Washington Boulevard,   CHICAGO

REV. R. IRA STONE
Superintendent of the Chicago Rescue Mission

Foreword

—

MY SOLE AIM in bringing this little pamphlet to you is to definitely call the attention of the men and women of the Central Western States, and especially those of the City of Chicago into whose hands it may come, to the vicious, thoroughly organized white-slave traffic of to-day, and its attendant, far-reaching, horrible results upon the young man and womanhood of our Land.

During a constant residence covering seven years of time in the central slum districts of the West and South Sides of Chicago, I have gained much actual knowledge of the questions of poverty, drink and prostitution among the lost men and women of these great neighborhoods, have become personally acquainted with very many of them, visiting them, listening to their heart stories and growing to know much of their inside lives, and have learned a real tender interest and pity for them in their remorseful, helpless, hopeless condition.

All incidents, references and statistics (as far as possible) herein given are strictly authentic, and have been collected with great care and fairness either by myself or my assistants.

Statistical references have been taken from the writings of United States Attorney Sims,

Rev. Ernest A. Bell and others engaged in prosecuting and reform work, all of whom I thank sincerely and wish well in what they are accomplishing for good where it is so desperately needed in this submerged underworld of our city.

———

So in bringing this eighth edition of CHICAGO'S BLACK TRAFFIC IN WHITE GIRLS to you, a part of which has already been published under the title of CHICAGO'S SOUL MARKET, it is the aim of the writer to give more thought and time to real, existing conditions—descriptions and actual facts relative to public prostitution and its attendant frightful results, rather than to such matter as incidents, "cases," etc., knowledge of which can usually be acquired by simply reading the daily press of Chicago or New York. All descriptions, statistics and photographs are taken by the author from actual contact with the great underworld and quoted with names, dates, etc., of those concerned and are absolutely authentic.

We, together with thousands of others— editors, legislators, club women, ministers and everybody else who has the welfare of the girlhood of our Land at heart, believe that the time for prudery and concealment is past and that honest men and women should know what there is to know about this thoroughly organized, solidly financed system of White Slavery flourishing and growing in America to-day—a system which controls and ruins hundreds of thousands

of women in our midst every year and which
requires a constant sacrifice of more than sixty
thousand young girls annually to feed its death
and disease dealing machinery.

Most people think of harlotry or prostitution as
something secret—something to be kept from the
public eye, something to be ashamed of.   Not
so to the great throng of Chicago whore-mongers.
Everything that can be done to attract attention
and custom is done by the five thousand men
and hundreds of hideous, brutish madams who
in this city exploit the bodies and live off the
earnings of thirty thousand public women in
our midst.   The twenty-seven hundred (quoting
from a statement of Chief of Police Stewart)
houses of ill-fame here are conducted with as
much publicity and advertising as the grocery
or meat market nearby.   Each adjoining and
nearby saloon, with its wine rooms and booths,
is an advertising and recruiting agency; the
ward politician, the officers on the beat, the
common "pimp" and the recognized whore-
mongers, work harmoniously together to exploit
this vast business.

Reckoning the number of White Slaves in
Chicago at thirty thousand, and the average
number of men entertained by each of these
unfortunate women nightly at five (a very low
average) with an average per man of one dollar,
there is poured monthly **Four Million Five
Hundred Thousand Dollars**, blood money, into
the coffers of these human dealers—as the
rental for profit of the bodies of our American

girl and her alien sister who has been mercilessly trapped, lured from her home and sold into the great festering cesspool, without the slightest knowledge of our customs and laws, and ruined forever.

New York City is the great eastern head-quarters and westward shipping point for Oriental and European White Slaves. Mark this statement:

"Seventeen hundred girls, by actual count, were lost on the way from New York to Chicago last year, according to an investigation now being made by the Commissioner of Immigration. Somehow these girls were spirited away from the care of the agents to whom they were entrusted and were never seen nor heard of again."

Isn't that an appalling fact? for fact it is—seventeen hundred girls lost and gone forever just from this one line of travel alone and in just one year! These girls, who came to this Country to better themselves, to make an honest living, broken and rotting to-day behind bolts and bars in some of our cities' foul dives, or else shipped on and on until at last in some Chinese underground cellar or under the lash of a South American or Philippine whore-master, Death at last comes to the rescue.

Please remember, as you read this, that America is becoming more and more un-American every day. Each ship, each train West-ward or Eastward bound, is now daily dumping into our Land, so lately the goal of the home-seeker from Germany, Sweden, Ireland, etc., the real future citizen—thousands of the scum and vice and criminal element of South Eastern Europe, Asia and the Orient, and remember too that a short five-years of residence here converts the filthiest criminal from Turkey, Arabia, Syria, Italy, or of any place else where vice and brutality reign supreme, into an American citizen with the right to vote into office men who will and are sworn to protect and aid in every possible way the Jewish, Russian, French or Chinese whore-master as he rents a shanty and proceeds to fatten on the very life-blood of the young girlhood of this and other lands.

JEAN TURNER-ZIMMERMANN, M. D.

The "Protected" White Slave Traffic.

Open prostitution—White Slavery, as it exists to-day in Chicago, is almost entirely under **foreign** control. Of the twenty-seven hundred houses of ill-fame in Chicago, a very large percentage are owned and controlled by foreigners from Southeastern Europe, while almost without exception all Levee and White Slave resorts in the segregated districts are under the direct ownership of the moral and civic degenerates of the French, Italian, Syrian, Russian, Jewish or Chinese races—once in a great while you may find a German or Swedish whore-master, but very seldom—an American or an Englishman conducting such a business is almost entirely unknown. American men raise the girlhood, make the laws and **elect** the officials whereby this bloody business may be carried on and exploited by a foaming pack of foreign hellhounds, who after their work of death is accomplished and their coffers filled, go home to their South Europe or Turkish haunts with their blood and soul money, to lives of filth and idleness in their own lands.

I appeal in the name of Jehovah, to the Church, to the women's clubs, to the labor federations and all honorable Jews and others of foreign birth who have come to America for a home and a decent, honorable living, to aid in every possible way the great work now going on to eradicate segregated, protected White Slavery from our Land.

EXTRACTS FROM THE DAILY PAPERS

Quoting from the Daily Press, May 4, regarding the recent investigations in New York concerning the question of White Slavery by the Rockefeller jury (which after buying two girls themselves, later declared, "there is no traffic in women in New York"):

Harry Levenson, the acknowledged "trader" of women who is in the Tombs under $25,000 bail, made a startling confession to the District Attorney to-night, giving names of men and women whose sole occupation is dealing in unfortunates.

"I know of three places in New York," Levenson said, "where five to ten girls are kept constantly at hand for sale. At any hour of the day or night one of them, two or the whole ten, can be bought by any one with the money to pay for them. They can be shipped anywhere at an hour's notice."

GIVES HINT ON ARRESTS

The "trader" gave to Mr. Whitman the addresses of the three places, which are known as "stockades." He also made suggestions as to how their operators might be apprehended.

More than that, Levenson told how the financial arrangements of the sales are made and how recruits are obtained.

Agents are continually at work obtaining young girls, the prisoner said. The slave sellers do not want hardened women, he explained; they want pretty, immature girls. The agents are generally well dressed women who ingratiate themselves with their childish victims at matinees and moving-picture shows, and by dining them and painting rosy pictures of a life of ease, win them away from their homes or their ill-paid positions.

"When there is a call for girls," Levenson continued, "the buyer hands over the money paid for them to the keeper. Then an agent—these are usually men—take the girls to wherever the "order" comes from. These agents then collect 10 per cent of the girl's weekly earnings."

Quoting from the National Prohibitionist, May 12:

THE SLAVE TRADE AND THE VOTER

The Christian voter who reads, and reads with blood boiling, as the blood of every honest man must, the shameful story of the exposure of the traffic in girls especially in New York, must not allow his imagination to run away with his reasoning faculties.

Awful as the story is, we invite attention, not to its horror—the horror of herds of little girls sold at a per-head price below the value of pigs—but to the practical questions of responsibility and cure.

Why does this infamy exist in our cities?

How can it exist?

Who is responsible?

The answers all come to one point—the governments that rule our cities.

The black and white wretches who are the immediate agents of vice are hardly worth considering.

They are mere incidents. Practically it is a waste of time to even prosecute them.

The trail of the real criminal leads into the police headquarters, leads up the steps of the city hall, goes across the threshold of the mayor's private office, enters the homes of Christian citizens and lies broad through the doors of the church.

For this infamy of the sale of innocent girls for vice and the whole wider, deeper, fouler vice system is a part of governmental policy, not in New York and Chicago alone, but all over the Country, under Republican and Democratic administration.

The very district attorney's office that exposes these particular instances of crime is one of the strong pillars of the system of which the crime is only an outcropping.

Even now there is not a voice lifted in official Chicago and New York in favor of doing the one thing that alone can stop the sale of girls, the one thing that the law clearly prescribes in the matter—wiping out the vice preserves, stopping the whole system of trade in vice. This fact needs to be burned deeply into the hearts of American voters: **If you want this thing to go on, if you want little girls still to be bought and sold like pigs, if you want pure young lives to be overwhelmed in fathomless shame, all you need to do to help keep up the system is to keep on voting for men who protect these criminals.**

Quoting from McClure's (July) Magazine concerning the recent investigation of the White Slave trade in New York City by a specially appointed jury:

In order to establish the existence of the White Slave traffic Assistant District Attorney James B.

Reynolds arranged to make actual purchases of girls in the Tenderloin and other sections of the underworld from those reputed to be large dealers. Skilled investigators who were not known in New York were engaged and put to work in the heart of the Tenderloin.

They were represented as purchasers of girls. Friendly and confidential relations were established with some of the most influential White Slave dealers. By these means valuable first-hand information was obtained regarding the White Slave trade. The agents were told the price of girls, the methods employed in the business, and, in some cases, the corrupt relations existing between the traders and certain officials.

Past and present conditions of the traffic were contrasted frequently, the trading during the present winter being described as exceptionally light because of the general alarm caused by the sitting of the "White Slave" Grand Jury. One large dealer told the agents that though two years ago he could have sold them all the girls they wanted at $5 or $10 apiece, he would not risk selling one in New York now for $1,000.

In spite of this general caution, purchases for cash were made of four girls, two through an East Side dealer, who boasted of formerly having made large sales in other cities, and two from a so-called black and tan dealer. Two of the girls are under 18.

.   .   .   With rare exceptions, not only the innocent women imported into this Country, but the prostitutes as well, are associated with men whose business it is to protect them, direct them, and control them, and who frequently, if not usually, make it their business to plunder them unmercifully. Now this system of subjection to a man has become common. The procurer or the pimp may put his woman into a disorderly house, sharing profits with the "madam". He may sell her outright; he may act as an agent for another man; he may keep her, making arrangements for her hunting men. She must walk the streets and secure her patrons, to be exploited, not for her own sake, but for that of her owner. Often he does not tell her even his real name. If she tries to leave her man, she is threatened with arrest. If she resists, she may be beaten; in some cases, when she has betrayed her betrayer, she has been murdered.

The ease and apparent certainty of profit has led thousands of our younger men, usually those of foreign birth or the immediate sons of foreigners, to abandon the useful arts of life to undertake the most accursed business ever devised by man.

Those who recruit women for immoral purposes watch all places where young women are likely to be found under circumstances which will give them a ready means of acquaintance and intimacy, such as picture shows, dance-halls, sometimes waiting rooms in large department stores, railroad stations, manicuring and hair dressing establishments.

The strongest appeal to the instincts of humanity in every right-minded person is made by a consideration of the brutal system employed by these traffickers to in every way exploit their victims, the hardened prostitute as well as the innocent maiden. It is probable that a somewhat larger proportion of the American girls are free from the control of a master; and yet, according to the best evidences obtainable—according to the stories of the women themselves and the keepers of the houses—nearly all the women now engaged in this business in our large cities are subject to pimps, to whom they give most of their earnings, or else they are under the domination of keepers of houses, a condition that is practically the same.

It is the business of the man who controls the women to provide police protection, either by bribing the police not to arrest her, or, in case of arrest, to secure bail, pay the fine, etc., to make all business arrangements, to decide what streets, restaurants, dance-halls, saloons and similar places she shall frequent.

There are large numbers of Jews scattered throughout the United States, although mainly located in New York and Chicago, who seduce and keep girls. Some of them are engaged in importation, but apparently they prey rather upon young girls whom they find on the street, in the dance-halls, and similar places, and who, by the methods already indicated—love-making and pretense of marriage—they deceive and ruin. Many of them are petty thieves, pickpockets and gamblers. They also have various resorts where they meet and receive their mail, and transact business with one another, and visit. Perhaps the best known organization of this kind throughout this Country was one legally incorporated in New York in 1904, under the name of the New York Benevolent Association.

It is, of course, difficult to prove by specific cases the relation of the police to this traffic, and to establish by specific evidence the fact generally accepted that the girls of disorderly house keepers regularly pay the police for protection; but high police officials, prosecuting officers, and social workers in all quarters assert that in many, if not all of our large cities, much corruption of this kind exists.

The importation and harboring of alien women and girls for immoral purposes and the practice of prostitution by them—the so-called "white slave traffic"—is the most pitiful and revolting phase of the immigration question. This business has assumed large proportions, and it has been exerting so evil an influence upon our Country that the Immigration Commission felt compelled to make it the subject of a thorough investigation.

The investigation was begun in November, 1907, under the active supervision of a special committee of the Immigration Commission; and the work was conducted by a special agent in charge, with numerous assistants.

The investigation has covered the cities of New York, Chicago, San Francisco, Seattle, Portland, Salt Lake City, Ogden, Butte, Denver, Buffalo, Boston and New Orleans.

There are between seven and eight hundred men in Seattle who live from the revenue from the "white slave traffic", almost all of whom could be reached by the State Courts, if proper efforts were made. It was established by the Grand Jury that the Federal Government has gone as far as the law allows. It is now up to the State authorities, who could break up this business in short order.

What are We Going to Do About the Children?

Levee women, women living in prostitution, "madams," etc., do not bring up their children (and most of Chicago's female dealers in

A Group of Children in the Midst of the "Red Light" District

prostitution have several of them) in or **near** segregated districts of vice. Like the saloon keeper who moved to Evanston to get his children away from the harmful, degenerating influences of the saloon and its environing neighborhoods, so the "madam," that active principal in the slavedom of the girls of our Land, in almost every case sees to it that **her** children are well brought up, away from the influences and knowledge of prostitution, while her agents and keepers are out scouring the department stores, factories, villages and country homes for girls to fill the sickening, festering, shrieking ranks of the great death army of publicly protected White Slaves.

The writer has investigated many cases, and in every instance has found the children of these vultures of girlhood in exclusive colleges or military schools, being excellently prepared to take decent positions in business and social life. Case after case has recently come to light of women supporting their children on the fashionable avenues, in Harvard and military colleges, while they themselves with hearts of hell, wring the dollars that pay for these luxuries from the bleeding, broken bodies of a gang of Levee White Slaves—your sister and mine—younger than her own, better born, better raised, but lost **forever** in the crushing, barred and screened gehenna of modern harlotry.

Sixty-nine per cent of the children raised in the vast slum neighborhoods surrounding the segregated districts of prostitution are ruined before reaching the age of eighteen. This dreadful, appalling feature has been recently brought to light through close investigation by the writer and her co-workers, together with the sickening fact that little girls scarcely more than babies, are being constantly sought, secured and sacrificed to satisfy the cravings of abnormal, degenerate vice and debauchery abounding in

every large city. These little children, painted
and showily dressed, are fast making their
appearance in such cities as New York and Chicago, and they are the forerunners of Oriental
child debauchery. These little girls are seldom
seen on the streets, but may be recognized when
seen, by their deformed, bowed legs, bent backs
and shrivelled little, old faces—such faces as we
find in cripples aged by pain. Our hearts have
been almost stilled as we have listened to the
terrible stories of the hundreds of little girls in
the ghastly fleshmarkets of India and China who,
by the knife and the insertion into their tender
bodies of wedges of expanding wood, are thus
made ready, through months of torture, for the
use of some inhuman Hindu or Chinese monster
who for the sum of a few dollars purchases the
use of their shrieking, quivering bodies, to leave
them after a day or two of unparalleled debauchery, dead, or if still living, then with broken
back or limbs, a human sacrifice indeed.

We have read and known all this and wished
that we could die that these children might be
saved—but listen, do we realize that with the
influx into our midst, into our larger cities, of
the vilest, most degenerate men and women on
earth, thousands upon thousands of the most
hellish brutes of Asia and China—men who
reckon girlhood lower than the female dog, has
come this very thing—this reeking, diabolical
crime against innocent girlhood. Two especially
revolting cases have come under the direct
notice of the writer, yet without sufficient legal

proof to face in court the organized, thoroughly financed band of men and women exploiting these dreadful conditions: one, a girl Louise, on Custom House Place; the other, Rosie from the 22nd Street environments. The last named, cut, torn and bleeding, made a statement to the writer that cannot be put in print; yet she was by her owners accused of masturbation. Both of these girls were under ten years of age.

The exploitation of women in Chicago in the vast business of White Slavery and segregated vice, is carried on very openly and above board. Street walkers carry on their nefarious business of securing trade for the "house" almost entirely unmolested. Women stand in the doors of the West Side houses of ill-fame and solicit those who pass.

At 737 Washington boulevard, two doors west of the Chicago Rescue Mission, with which the writer is connected, a woman* stands in the door constantly soliciting each male passer-by; boys are invited to come in and take their first lesson in vice, and on this block are many, many children, boys and girls. One of the "girls" kept by this woman was a harlot known as "No-nose" whose whole face was so sunken with syphilis that her nose was almost gone. The writer remembers well when through the efforts of a fellow-worker "No-nose" was sent to the County Hospital for medical treatment, and considers this girl one of the greatest

---

* Through the effort of the writer and the aid of the agent of the building this woman was made to move a little further west.

menaces to Chicago boyhood. No man would have touched the woman.

The blocks in this immediate vicinity are all thickly peopled by families with many children in them. The following group of little girls live in their alley-homes within a few doors of some of the worst sights and dives in Chicago.

Children of the Slums

They see no sights but vice, they hear no talk but filth. At the age of ten they are perfectly familiar with all the ins and outs of harlotry, know many prostitutes, many pimps.

Do you think these girls (each one is known to the writer personally) have any chance for virtue?

At 804 Washington Boulevard, almost across the street from the writer's office, appears the following sign on the window of the cigar store located there.

Hundreds of the wreckage of typical White Slavery pass this place daily, for it is located at the edge of the great West Side dumping ground for broken, diseased women and young girls whose bodies can no longer be profitably used in the higher class dives of the South Side segregated districts, and who must at the end of a year or two become, if they are still living, the notorious women of the night who walk the streets and alleys, selling the use of their vile bodies for twenty-five cents, ten cents, a drink of beer or a crust of free lunch, becoming the prey of the drunken bum, the low vicious foreigner, the negro, or else the ruination of every young boy who falls into their vulture-like clutches.

In all Chicago there could not be a generally worse neighborhood than the one in which the White Slave Cigar is manufactured and advertised for sale. Within a few blocks of the factory, which is two doors west of the corner of Washington Boulevard and Halsted Street, there are a thousand broken, pitiful lost White Slaves.

Within two or three blocks of this corner, five typical White Slaves have been murdered (butchered would be a better word) within the space of just a few weeks. Here drunken women, the outcast element of the better class of dives, trail their filthy bodies day and night, their sunken, half-starved, syphjletic faces staring in your face, seeking the man or the young boy who will give them a drink of whiskey or a crust of bread in return for the wretched commerce they have to offer. Here, too, the children play and little girls grow into big girls with scarcely a ghost of a chance to be decent, and facing all hangs the sign "White Slave Cigar," manufactured by George F. Walz.

It is out of this great outlaw district, this vast West Side charnal house of harlotry, that the City gets its supply of girls for that class of vice known as degeneracy.

Five years of work in prostitution constitutes the life of the average harlot. Many, before the time allotted to them in a life of ill-fame expires, die; many commit suicide, yet some live on, their diseased bodies constituting that class of girls known as street walkers and degenerates. These women, who are really only young girls, hang around the back rooms and cellars of the barrel houses, consorting with the drunken, crippled, diseased men who congregate in such places, and from this vast army of lost girlhood is supplied the material for the immoral Oriental shows abounding in the segregated districts, where with dogs and burros, the bodies of ruined, diseased girls are finally used up and destroyed, or in the bestial dives in which are practiced that horrible crime known as the "French method."

Sixty-nine per cent of the little girls who must, through necessity and environment, grow up in the neighborhoods immediately surrounding the segregated vice districts of such cities as Chicago, New York, Seattle, etc., are ruined before they reach the age of eighteen years. Think of it! These children know little else than drink and prostitution, hear little else, see little else. To them harlotry is in all its blasting, withering phases, a familiar story before they have reached the age of ten years. Hundreds of whore mongers, panderers, pimps and outlawed harlots, exploit their awful business and tell their vile stories as they walk the same pathway day by day with these children—little lost souls they are—the children of the poor, looked on in pity though by one who said "Inasmuch as ye have done it unto the least of these, ye have done it unto Me."

THE TRANSIENT HOTEL EVIL.

In this vast underworld another trap almost as dangerous as the house of prostitution abounds on every hand—the so-called "hotel"— really a mere house of assignation in almost every instance. These hotels are a constant menace to the girlhood of our Land—girls who come to the city strangers, and are unable to discriminate between the good and bad. Dozens of these hotels flourish all around the districts of vice in our cities, the abiding place of the pimp, the beggar, the criminal, and yet flourish under complete political protection. We sincerely believe that the time for cleaning up has come in such cities as New York, Chicago, etc., and we believe that we have with us in this stand, not only decent Chicago and New York, but decent America.

CRUSADE AGAINST "WHITE SLAVERY."

Thirteen governments have signed the international agreement to fight the traffic in women for immoral purposes. The terms have just been announced at Ottawa, Canada.

The list of countries, British colonies and protectorates which have decided to adhere to the Anti-White Slave Traffic Agreement are: Austria-Hungary, Belgium, Brazil, Denmark, France, Germany, Great Britain, Italy, Norway, Sweden, Portugal, Russia, Spain, Switzerland, the Bahamas, Barbadoes, British Guiana, Canada, Ceylon, Australia, Gambia, Gold Coast, Malta, Newfoundland, Northern Nigeria, Southern Rhodesia, Trinidad and the Windward Islands.

The End of the Way. Where Young Girls, who attend Public Dances and
Other Places of Amusement Unattended, are
Likely to Wind Up

Escape from a Life of Prostitution is Almost Impossible

After more than four years of experience, and after having visited in various capacities, disguised, etc., many of the worst haunts of vice and houses of prostitution in Chicago, I have personally come to this conclusion:

There is but a small chance for a girl, once having been sold into or entered upon a life of prostitution, to ever escape therefrom. Invariably she is kept in debt to her masters; excessive bills for parlor clothes, board, dentistry, laundry and all conceivable expenses are kept charged up against her. She is under constant threat of personal violence and blackmail in every form (her owners securing whenever possible, some knowledge of her home and friends, and continually holding this knowledge as a dagger over her), and there is the ever-present whoremasters and madams with drugs, drinks and bolts and bars, guarding every avenue of escape with blows and curses and brutality beyond conception. Very few young girls enter a life of prostitution voluntarily, and few, having once entered, ever escape therefrom.

A WORD OF PROTEST

The writer just here wishes to enter vigorous protest against houses of prostitution in Chicago and in **America** furnishing the American girl or her alien sister for the use of that class of alien men who are either excluded from citizenship in our Country by law, or who without wife or family, are here temporarily and simply to make all the money possible, in as short a time and in any way possible.

At 2130 Armour Avenue, Chicago, stands an old tenement house filled with girls—girls from all over the United States—a beautiful ruined girl from Georgia, girls from Europe. Good girls they were a year or two ago, but are now the chained, wrecked slaves of festering vice and habit. This place is said to be operated by a dope-fiend by the name of W—— and is exclusively for the use of a class of men debarred from the United States by law, except for educational purposes and mercantile interests among their

own kind, a class of men with whom no white
laborer will live or work—the class of men who
a year or two ago murdered Elsie Siegel in New
York—the lop-shouldered, smuggled-in, pig-
tailed opium parched Chinese. It is a crying
shame to-day against our Churches, our Union
Labor and our Law that there is allowed to
exist on a public street, in the second city in the
United States, a public stock-market for wrecked
girlhood where the filthy Chinese, in rows, wait
their turn to rent for thirty minutes of unparalleled Asiatic debauchery, the bruised, bleeding
wreckage of our American home or the girl
who came to us a few months ago—to the greatest Christian Republic the World has ever builded,
from some European home and a mother, asking only a chance to go to work with her bare
hands and earn a decent living.

The American citizen refuses to admit the
Chinaman, refuses to work with him, refuses
him all rights accorded other aliens coming to
us, and yet, for the blood profits of vice and
politics, allows to be placed to his exclusive
privilege that which a short time ago was our
Nation's best and cleanest womanhood.

———

For an American girl entering a life of public
prostitution there is some chance of salvation,
for the immigrant girl there is indeed little.
Two years ago I had occasion to visit 21—
Armour Avenue, a "50-cent house" in the
infamous "bedbug row district." It was about
three o'clock in the afternoon, just before the

beginning of regular business hours. In the reception room of the place, around a rusty old stove, sat eight or ten hopeless, lost girls; sick, smoking, cursing girls. Soon they would dress up, dope up with whiskey, cocaine or opium, dash some bella donna in their eyes and go on duty to meet all comers. Shivering by the stove sat a little foreign girl. I asked her name, the girls told me it was Josie and that she was an Italian. Speaking to her in that language, I soon learned that she was a young Russian Jewess. The house seemed to possess sufficient proof, as the law then required, that the girl had been in this Country three years; so there was little I could do except give her my card and tell her if she ever needed a friend to come to me. Less than a year ago there came a ring at my door, and opening it, I found a lost woman begging me to come at once into the West Side "levee" to see a girl who was dying. I went with her, and there, in a mouldy, wretched cellar I found "Josie" of the Armour Avenue resort, dying with syphilis. In that awful underground place I listened to her story and I give it to you as she related it to me:

"I am nineteen years old and my name is Gezie Bruvatsky. I saw my father bayonetted to the earth by Russian soldiers. I saw my mother work over the washtub until her hands were bloody that I and my little brother might have bread and my virtue be protected. One day a man came to our house, who was either a Jew or a German, saying he was agent for a steamship company and that he had good work in America for many girls where they could earn as much in one month, as they could earn in two years in Russia. My heart leaped with joy. How could we know he was lying. I packed my clothes. I left all—my mother, my brother. I came to America. Soon I could send for them, for I was strong and could work--work day and night. At New York a man and woman met me and sent me on to Chicago. Here I was taken from the Polk Street Station to Armour Avenue where by force I was ruined. I was there many months, sick and starving, and finally got out and crawled over to the West Side where there are many Jews; but now I am dying and I want my mother."

WHAT THE U. S. PROSECUTING ATTORNEY SAYS:

Hon. Edwin Sims, ex-U. S. Prosecuting Attorney, in a recent conservative statement, says he believes that **fifteen thousand** immigrant girls are brought into this Country every year for commercialized prostitution.

We believe the actual figures are nearer Twenty-five Thousand, and we appeal to the mothers and fathers of America, in the name of God and the heart-broken mothers and fathers of other lands, to use their personal influence and the money with which God has entrusted them, to wipe from our flag the leprous blotch of shame which permits the importing in' our Republic every year of thousands of helpless girls to be ground up in the murder mills of the segregated harlotry of such districts as the 22nd Street district of Chicago, for it was the blood-covered hand of that district that reached across the lands and seas and into that

Russian home and tore from it little Gezie
Bruvatsky and led her across the waters and
under the very shadow of the Statue of Liberty
itself and pinning to her the little blue ticket of
immigration, led her past the gates of Ellis
Island, on past the statues of Washington and
Jefferson, of Lincoln and Grant, and into the
burning fire of American public prostitution to
live a few months, and dying in an underground
cellar, be cast, scarce cold, into our nation's
great potter's field of lost women.

**The Wretched, Pitiful Ending of Gezie Bruvatsky, left by Her Heartless
Masters to Die Unattended in Filthy, Squlid Surroundings**

The Price of a Living Body

Fifty years ago, down in the Southland of our America, we stood a well formed, sound limbed, healthy, intact young woman on the auction block and sold her to the highest bidder for her beauty, her virtue, her heart, her honor, her soul and her body, and the established average price paid for such a young woman was eighteen hundred dollars ($1800.00). I take for granted as I write, that if the heart and soul and body of a young black woman of Kentucky, Georgia or Mississippi was in the slave market of fifty years ago worth intrinsically $1800.00, the soul and body of a clean, decent, young Northland white woman is to-day worth about the same. Assistant State Prosecuting Attorney Roe in his speech before the Illinois Vigilance Society, Chicago, February 7th, 1909, placed the number of women in disorderly resorts in Chicago alone at 30,000.

Stop! Listen: If there are 30,000 young women on this City's Soul-Market, and we place the average value of one of these young women at $1,800, AND WE CERTAINLY DO PLACE IT THERE, by established, recognized precedent, then there is $54,000,000 worth of young womanhood in the Slave-Market of our City at the present time. In the same statistical speech Mr. Roe places the number of young girls necessary yearly to recruit the rapidly decimating ranks of this vast Death Army at six thousand; hence, $10,800,000 worth of innocent girlhood must be sacrificed from our stores and factories, our homes or firesides all over the Land every twelve months to feed and satisfy the horrible flesh-market of Human Slavery in the "levee" districts of Chicago alone.

Harry A. Parkin, Assistant U. S. District Attorney, in WOMEN'S WORLD, March, 1909, says:

"The Federal investigations in Chicago and other localities have clearly established the fact that, generally speaking, houses of ill-fame in large cities do not draw their recruits to any great extent from the territory immediately surrounding them; for various reasons the White Slavers who are the recruiting agents of this vile traffic prefer to work in States more or less distant from the centers to which victims are destined."

In view of all this, it must be clearly apparent that the need of the hour is legislation which will make it as difficult and dangerous for a White Slaver to take his victim from one State into another as it is to bring them from France, Italy, Canada or any other foreign country, to a house of ill-fame in Chicago or any American city. Therefore, it is suggested that if each State in the Union would enact and enforce laws against this importation, this terrible traffic would be dealt a blow in its most vulnerable part.

One of the strangest results brought about by the recent White Slave prosecutions in Chicago and the wide publicity which they have received has been the astonishment of thousands of persons, as evidenced by letters, at the fact that such a wholesale traffic is actually in existence, but what is still more astounding, not to say discouraging, is the reluctance of other thousands to believe that many hundreds of men and women are actually engaged in the business of luring young girls and women to their destruction and that this infamous traffic is being carried on in every state of the Union every day of the year.

It is estimated by those who should know, that at least five thousand men in Chicago live off of the earnings of prostitution. For instance as to the plan: A young girl, alien or American, is sold into a life of ill-fame for say Two Hundred Dollars, as the actual price of her procuring. Before she suspects any real harm, she is lured into a restaurant or a wine-room, becomes intoxicated, is sufficiently doped to become passive, is taken to the "house" to which she has been consigned and is immediately "broken in" in the most violent and nauseating manner, perhaps becoming the prey of twenty or thirty men. Beaten, threatened with exposure, and, if necessary, purposely infected with gonorrhea, the girl is within twenty-four hours absolutely ruined for all time—"spoiled," the police say. Oh! what a whole world of agony and pain and bruises and disease and Hell is embodied in that one word "spoiled." She is immediately pressed into service and from that time on until death relieves her, or she is rescued by some one enough interested to help her, she must receive all comers THIRTY DAYS every month.

This answers the question I have been asked a hundred times from all over the Country since CHICAGO'S SOUL MARKET was first published, as to whether a woman in a house of prostitution is allowed any respite from service during the Menstrual Period. SHE IS NOT ALLOWED A SINGLE DAY. The average number of men who must be served by each woman in a medium or lower class house of ill-fame is thirty-six per day. On entrance to the place, if the house be a "Dollar house," a metal room-check is purchased from the madam or attendant at the door for one dollar. This check is taken up by the girl in the room and is worth on presentation to the house fifty cents, half of its face value being received by the house for board, laundry, hair dressing, etc., all of which must be paid for at the highest possible rates. Of the remaining fifty cents, twenty-five cents goes to the man who sold the girl into the house, the remaining twenty-five cents going to the girl herself and from this amount must be paid all bills for clothes, dentistry, and all other expenses. In almost every known case, however, with which the writer is at all familiar, the entire fifty per cent goes intact to the owner of the girl, her necessary expenses being paid by him and the balance pocketed for his own use.

Just as the liquor trade is thoroughly and carefully financed and organized even in its weakest points, making successful prosecution against it a thing impossible, just so is the traffic in young women protected in all its details. The writer has in mind the case of Josie E——, fifteen years old, who came from her suburban home in Illinois, hoping to secure employment in the City. Arriving at the Dearborn Street Railway Station about nine o'clock, she started out to find a hotel in which to spend the night. Walking a few steps from the Station, she was accosted at State and Polk streets by a young man who asked her what she was looking for. Replying that she was looking for a hotel, the man Thompson told her he was employed at a hotel on Polk Street opposite the railway station and offered to take the girl there. Unacquainted with the City and relying on his word, she accompanied him to the hotel, where she was outraged and detained for weeks. She was finally rescued by the writer and a Y. W. C. A. worker. Taking her to my rooms, I found her physical condition such that I sent for a detective from the Harrison Street Police Station who investigated her story and finding it true in every particular, arrested Thompson at his place of employment, 41 Polk Street. The case coming up in the Harrison Street Municipal Court, was so manipulated by the defense that in the transferring of it to the Criminal Court a technical error threw it out altogether. I simply give this as an example of how almost utterly impossible it is to secure a conviction in these cases. Is it any wonder when back of this great evil stands at least a hundred million dollars?

Listen, seventy-five per cent of the women and girls entering lives of ill-fame in Chicago are from adjoining States and country districts— they are utter strangers in our City. Every hour, day or night, year in and year out, four great central railway passenger stations discharge their precious human freight within the first ward of Chicago, the richest and wickedest political ward in the world—the ward of Michael Kenna (Hinky Dink) and "Bathhouse" John Coughlin—the ward feeding every district of prostitution and gambling and unnatural horror in the City—the ward with two miles of indecent resorts, whole armies of reeking lost women, hundreds of pandering men procurers and White Slavers—the ward of thousands of Turkish, Italian and Arabian immigrants, and opium-parched pagan Chinese—the ward in which every day thousands of women, many of whom without money or friends, are looking for work, are unloaded in this seething cauldron of vice, their only refuge being, when without funds, the Police Station or the house of ill-repute.

The horror of conditions surrounding a woman without money or friends in Chicago makes the living of a moral life almost impossible for her. I have in mind the case of a deserted little Italian woman, G. P——, living in Plymouth Court, south of Polk Street. G. had three little baby girls, the eldest only four years, and was expecting another child soon. She was deserted by her husband and left without a dollar or a friend to face life and care for herself and babies. The case came into the hands of the Mission and she was cared for by them until the

N.B.—G. P.'s is strictly authentic. The Chicago Rescue Mission will give you details and take charge of any help you may care to give her.

time of her confinement, when, with her children, she was taken to Dunning Poorhouse
where she was kindly cared for. A baby boy
was born to G. Great pressure was brought to
bear upon this little Italian mother who spoke
no word of English, to induce her to give up her
children. Frightened and weeping, she refused
to do this, declaring she would make a living for
them, and leaving the Poorhouse, she started out
taking the baby and another child with her,
hoping soon to earn the money to care for the
other two.

This she was fortunate enough to accom-
plish, and, taking the four little ones dear to
her heart, went back to the little room on the
top floor of the tenement in Plymouth Court.
G. got work in a sweatshop and made button-
holes at $2.50 a week. She worked hard to keep
up, but the baby sickened and died. The other
children began to get thin and wan. They grew
hungry before her eyes and the mother's heart
frightened and sank within her. A fiend in
human form, J. F——, came by and offered the
half-starved mother bread for herself and babies,
offered her marriage as soon as it could be
arranged for. G. took the bread and fed her
children and to-day up on the top floor of the
tenement in Plymouth Court, again deserted and
hungry and helpless, she cries and prays and
makes button-holes, and waits and waits with
fear and wretchedness the coming of another
little child.

The proprietor of the great resort on the
corner of 21st and Dearborn streets said not

From a flashlight photograph showing 2-ton weight
steel door connecting sound-proof dungeon cell
with blind passage-way, between 114
and 116 Custom House Place

long ago to a co-worker of mine who forced her way into his infamous dive:

"Don't come here to bother my girls; it is of no use; they are rotten and ripe for H——. Soon I will throw them out myself. Go to the department stores and the sweatshops and help the underpaid, friendless girl *there* if you must work. I could write a book as large as that (pointing to the City Directory) filled with shrieks and groans of women *after they are lost,* but what good would it do? They are gone then *forever.*"

In a great measure, the man told the truth. It is hard to reach a woman after she has once entered a life of prostitution; for, like the Inferno of old, there should be emblazoned in letters of blood above the barred door of every White Slave mart in America, the ancient warning:

"Leave hope behind, all ye who enter here."

There's many a girl homeless and tempted, underpaid and destitute, who might be saved from a life of ill-fame if a helping hand and a shelter were offered her in her hour of indecision and hunger and despair.

In the south wall of the basement of 114 Federal Street, formerly known as Custom House Place, that congested, central Redlight District of three years ago, there was a blind passage-way between 114 and 116 Custom House Place, 116 being the notorious dive "The California" now located at —— Armour Avenue. On the inside, this door opened into a large dungeon, windowless, sound-proof (about 7x10 feet) and it is alleged that it was through the alley and

From a flashlight photograph showing heavy steel
screen used inside the iron-barred windows
of the houses of prostitution in the
old Custom House district

into this blind passage-way that the unwilling victims of White Slavers (the same syndicate now operating with Chicago as headquarters) were carried into this little solitary cell to be "broken in" by fiendish, brute force to a life of shame.

The accompanying photograph secured by the writer gives at least a faint idea of this frightful trap against the pitiless walls of which have, no doubt, beat the agonized shrieks of many an innocent girl—your sister and mine—as, baptising this hell-hole with blood and tears, her quivering body was crucified upon a whoremonger's cross of gold and then torn down to be cast, bruised, bleeding, but yet alive, into five years of the awful, seething moral Golgotha of prostitution and then into **lingering death.**

The Chicago Rescue Mission and Woman's Shelter of which the writer is President, has for two years occupied the premises at 114 Custom House Place. Upon moving into the place we found every window incased in heavy iron bars while between the bars and the glass of each window was mortised a one-half inch steel screen (see cut). Entrance or exit from the building was as utterly impossible as from a penitentiary, excepting by the **front door,** and to bring the place within the requirements of the City law it was necessary to bring a suit through the Municipal Court against the owner of the building, Mrs. Spiegel, against whom through the aid of Assistant Prosecuting Attorney Oleson, we obtained a verdict and forced her thereon to put in a rear stairway (see Court records).

114 Custom House Place is only one of the fifty similarly notorious dens in the old Redlight district, and yet it is impossible to make some people believe that there is such a thing as forcible detention of a woman in a Chicago house of prostitution.

FROM THE "WOMAN'S WORLD"

I quote the following incident cited by Assistant Prosecuting Attorney Roe in an article of recent date in WOMAN'S WORLD, illustrating some of the schemes and plans for leading a girl into a life of ill-fame. Mr. Roe says:

"A year ago last summer, 15-year old Margaret Smith was working about her simple home near Benton Harbor, Michigan. The father, employed by the Pere Marquette Railroad, was away from home a good share of the time. One day a graphophone agent came to the house and the family became interested in one of his musical machines. Shortly afterward this agent brought with him to the Smith home Frank Kelly, and introduced him to Maggie, as she was called by her folks. In a day or two Margaret was on her way to Chicago with Kelly who promised her an excellent position in the City. Upon her arrival Margaret was sold to one of the worst dives in Chicago, located on South Clark Street and owned by an Italian named Baptista Pizza. Here she learned that her captor's name was not Frank Kelly, but an Italian whose real name is Alphonso Citro. For a year she was kept as a Slave in this resort, which was over a saloon, and the entrance was through a back alley. The only visitors were Italians, who came for immoral purposes. Learning last summer that Margaret's father, who had been hunting relentlessly for his daughter, was on the track of her, the girl was taken by Alphonso Citro, alias Kelly, to Gary, Indiana. When the father came to the resort with a policeman, he found that his daughter had gone. She was kept in Gary about two months and then returned to this disreputable place from which she escaped finally, the Monday before last Christmas. A young barber took pity on her after hearing her story, and enlisted the sympathies of his parents who took her to their home. Alphonso Citro (Kelly) looked for her almost a week, and at last saw her going from a store to this home, where she was staying. He went to the house and demanded at the point of a revolver that she be given up, as he said:

"I am losing money every day she is gone."

"There was a quarrel over the girl during which some people from the outside were attracted to the house by the commotion. Citro, becoming frightened, fled down the street, and as he ran, threw away the revolver with which he had tried to shoot the father of the barber during the quarrel, over the fence into a coal yard. After running two blocks, he was caught and arrested. Upon these facts this procurer, Citro, alias Kelly, was prosecuted and found guilty under the new pandering law of Illinois, and received a sentence of one year of imprisonment and a fine of five hundred dollars. The poor father and mother, distressed and heart-broken, were in Court during the trial with their arms around each other, sobbing with joy because their little girl had been found. Pizza, the owner of the place, was indicted by the State grand jury, but escaped to Italy. This case is told to show how girls leave home upon the promise of securing employment and are in this way procured for places of ill-repute."

NOTE.—Baptista Pizza, it was discovered, did not go to Italy, but after a few months of hiding, again engaged in his nefarious business. He was recently arrested for selling an American girl, fined $1000.00 and sentenced to two years in the House of Correction.

Chicago's Soul Market.

"O, he keeps a bunch of 'fillies' in a shanty down near the corner of Monroe and Peoria streets, and they're not foreigners, either. They're American girls. No wonder he can make a bet like that on a mere chance, from a roll of yellow backs."

The speaker was the madam of a Peoria street resort, the listeners, a motley crowd of women gathered in the rear of a popular saloon and gambling house not far from the corner of Green and Madison streets, on the seething, congested West Side of Chicago. These women had assembled in that screened back room to risk their hard earned or evil-gotten money on the horses of the Louisville race track.

There sat a little 18-year old, brown-eyed milliner, her dissipated face hollow and drawn from worry and lack of sleep and an insufficient quantity of nourishing food, while near her a white-haired old lady in shabby black was tightly grasping two quarters, her entire worldly possession. Just across sat a well-dressed woman restaurant keeper, a young eastern star and half a hundred others, above all of whom shone the yellow haired madam of the Peoria Street resort, the star patron of that great gambling room for women, each one of whom was eagerly beckoning the well-groomed bookmaker, feverishly anxious to get her pittance on the race-track favorite, when a connecting door was pushed suddenly open and in rushed a fashionably dressed, brutal-faced young Russian

Jew, holding loosely an immense roll of money. Tens, twenties, hundreds—he counted them until three hundred dollars had been placed to win upon a "clocker tip" in that day's last race in Louisville.

There was grim, deadly silence—eating, unbearable silence in that gambling room as they waited the ring of the telephone and the name of the winner. Again the yellow haired madam's voice screamed shrilly out, for she was indeed ill at ease, her money was all on the favorite—"Yes, a bunch of American 'fillies' peddled out at 50 cents an hour to all comers, black or white, sick or sound. No wonder he can make a play like that on an outside chance."

Three-hundred dollars! My heart stood still almost. The thought flashed through my brain that that wager meant hundreds of hours of shame and slavery and horror to those girls in the shanties down on Peoria street, some mother's girl, every one of them. I sat still for a little while and watched the feverish anxious throng about me. My heart kept going faster and faster until I could bear it no longer. American "fillies" and body and soul under a brutal Russian whore-monger! I slipped quietly out into the street; night was coming on, and I walked down Madison and south on Peoria. Yes, there were the shanties—poor, wretched hovels, every one of them. Out shone the flickering red lights, out came the discordant, rasping sound of the rented piano, out belched the

shrieks and groans of drunken harlots mingled
with the curses of task-masters in a foreign
tongue, attracting the attention of the hundreds
of laborers, negroes and boys, as they walked
home on Peoria street from their day's work.
On I went until I came to a little shed just north
of the slum saloon occupied by one Shellstadt
at the corner of Monroe and Peoria streets, and
checking my steps, I looked around me on the
squalid, wretched scene. I was in the midst of
prostitution at its lowest—the heart-breaking
dregs of Chicago's thirty thousand public
women. Yes, there they were—the fair young
American girl, the stolid Russian Jewess, the
middle-aged, syphiletic harlot, living, prosti-
tuting, dying like so many hurt, broken moths
around that great red-light—Chicago's West
Side Soul Market—their poor, wrecked, foul
smelling bodies sold day and night at from
twenty-five to fifty cents an hour to all comers
who could pay the pitiful price demanded by
their brutal, soulless masters; and, as I looked,
the burning fire of intense pity entered my soul
for these drug and drink-sodden, diseased and
chained slaves—my sisters in Christ and this
great, free American Republic, and so, with a
heart-consuming desire to know more of the
lives of these scarlet women and to help them, if
possible, I began at once a thorough personal
investigation of Chicago's public Slave Market,
visiting these people whenever occasion offered;
talking with them, gaining their much abused
confidence, until I gradually learned the inside
lines of the saddest story America has ever

known, since the black mothers of our Southland were torn from their black and white babies and with shrieks of agony and heart strings bleeding and soul rent with blackened horror were sold to death on the plantations of Louisiana and Mississippi, and I want to tell you who read this and who think there is little truth in the now much agitated question of White Slavery in America, that in the dives and dens of our City's underworld I have heard shrieks and heart cries and groans of agony and remorse that have never been surpassed at any public slave auction America has ever witnessed, as these girls, many of them, oh! so young, realizing their awful fate, with scalding tears and moans of horror, shut out from their hearts and lives father or mother or husband and child, and turned their sob-shaken, tortured bodies to face the years of final, relentless wretchedness and woe, to be at last thrown out sick and broken, to die in some alley or to be carted off to Dunning poorhouse to gradual physical decay and a pauper's burial and grave of obliteration, while those who sold them just a few years before go out in their diamonds and fine linen and their great automobiles to buy up more girls (it might be your daughter, father, mother; or it might be mine) to fill the vacancy in the ranks of this vast army of White Slaves.

A woman said to me the other day, and it was in a lofty, sneering tone, too: "I doubt if these women are ever coerced or even imposed upon."

LISTEN; READ, THEN LISTEN.

Sitting in my office one afternoon I listened, my blood almost freezing, to the following story vouched for by Mr. C——, an immigration inspector and brother of a well-known Chicago reform worker. Here it is as he told it to me:

"One evening some time ago I was looking up a case down in the Twenty-Second Street red-light district, and visited and inspected, looking for immigrant girls held illegally, a certain house of the lower class in that neighborhood of prostitution. While in the house I noticed a young woman lying very ill (in the last stages of pneumonia, if I remember the story exactly) and in a semi-conscious condition, and to my horror upon inquiry I learned that in the rush hours of business this helpless, pain-racked young woman was *open to all comers* holding an accredited room check."

Dear friends, there are true stories heard and known every day around the City's seething, blood-red Soul Market that cannot be put into print—stories, though, that were they to become known, would make decent Chicago rise as one man and cry with a voice outspeaking Fort Sumter, "White Slavery in Chicago and in America must cease!"

During my years of study of this question of prostitution I learned to know personally many of the characteristic White Slaves of the West and South Side "levees." One "Alice" I shall never, never forget. Beautiful aside from her dissipation, a high school graduate, grammar and syntax perfect, manner exquisite. "Alice," seduced at eighteen, was at the age of twenty-one away down the line in the West Side levee underworld. I used to talk many times with Alice as she sat in the back parlor of the "house" on Peoria street that gave her shelter, awaiting her call of "next" to go up stairs with whosoever—negro, white or Chinese—might buy for one dollar (one of the dollars of the Republic on which is eternally stamped the blessed words, "In God we Trust") possession of her beautiful body for one hour. Smoking, always smoking her doped Turkish cigarette, Alice told me much of her life, both in years gone forever and of a daily "levee" existence. She told me of a father and mother and a beautiful home, of a lover who came into it and led her away by night into "levee" Slavery—of the awful disgrace and disinheritance, of a little baby that she only knew an hour, of insane remorse and anguish, until at last she would stand and scream and scream with mental pain until some whoremonger knocked her senseless, and then how she would crawl away to some near-by shanty saloon and drink herself helpless, to forget.

As far as I know Alice is still on Peoria street, and, oh! men and women, there are thirty thousand of these Alices in Chicago's great blasting Soul Market to-day.

United States Attorney Sims puts the average life of a prostitute at ten years or less, while other excellent authorities put it as low as five years, as these women must constantly drink any and all drinks purchased for them by visitors (as much of the business revenue is derived from the sale of these drinks), thus forcing them at all times into a half-drunken condition, rendering them helpless to control the abnormal, sickening, mind and body wrecking demands made upon them by the gonorrheal, syphilitic, sodden wretches of whom not one in ten is capable of normal sexual coalition, yet whose debauched, drunken desires and requirements, no matter how unnatural and revolting, must be satisfied by the use of the bodies of their hopeless victims at fifty or even as low as twenty-five cents an hour.

Very few young women entering this cesspool of prostitution are able to live therein an average of eight weeks without becoming infected with one or more of the loathsome diseases of the underworld, and thus ruined and horrible they live on and on for three, four or six years, and at the end of that time thirty thousand pure young girls, gathered from prairie homes and village firesides and from out of our own suburban and city families, must march out into this great Soul Market to take the place of the broken wretches whose decaying bodies are cast into the refuse of our alleys and sewers to become the menace of every girl and boy and drunken man who comes within their clutches or sets foot within their alley hovels.

THE END OF THE WAY.

At about ten o'clock on Saturday evening, September 19th, I boarded a West Madison

street car and, transferring north at Halsted
street, alighted at Lake and walked west to
Lewinsky's saloon at the corner of Lake and
Green streets. Going around to the side entrance
on Green street, I discovered in the wine and
back rooms of the wretched place a crowd of
perhaps fifty drunken, dirty, diseased men and
women, most of them foul-smelling, young white
girls huddled in with the worst mob of negroes,
whites and Chinese I have seen in Chicago's
slums, all cursing, drinking, singing and blas-
pheming in plain view and hearing of the street.
I stopped a moment to make sure I was making
no mistake in what I saw and then crossed the
street to interview the dark-eyed little foreign
girl who at its door was boldly soliciting trade
for the saloon and its adjacent evils, just
opposite.

I walked on down to Peoria and south on that
notorious street.

In the row of houses running from Lake to
Randolph street there are approximately six
hundred White Slaves, and diseased, crippled
prostitutes of the lowest class, dumped from the
city's cleaner dives, and on that night it was
almost impossible to push one's way through
the mass of men and boys—whites, negroes,
Turks, Polocks, etc., gathered in front of these
places of public abomination. At the corner of
Randolph and Peoria streets several earnest men
and women were holding a little gospel meeting,
and, stopping with them, I counted during the
thirty minutes I stayed there six hundred and

forty (approximately) men and boys stop in front of or enter this horrible flesh market.

As I left the scene, a young girl in a drunken, filthy, diseased condition slipped out of an alley and followed me, asking me to help her, and as we sat on the steps of Saints Peter and Paul Cathedral, corner of Washington boulevard and Peoria street, she told me the worst, most heart-breaking story of wrong and vice and ruin I have ever listened to (see note.)*

As I left that West Side levee of vice I knew I had seen prostitution at its lowest ebb and that from these holes of horror finally went those awful alley women of the night to sell their soul and trail their black disease to any young boy or drunken man who could give them a few cents or even the price of a drink of whiskey.

Coming down Custom House Place one night about 10:30 o'clock I overtook, without their knowledge, six boys, ranging from about twelve down to perhaps seven years, three of whom I knew fairly well. Following them from shadow to shadow, I gathered sufficient of their low-voiced conversation to make me certain they had been holding an orgy in a nearby cellar or base-ment with a drunken harlot, and that together they had paid her the small sum of seventeen cents for this damning, soul-destroying com-merce. One boy, a lad of about nine years, had

---

*This girl was turned over to the Chicago Rescue Mission, cleaned and clothed and fed and pointed to Jesus Christ. Her story was investigated and found true and after receiving medical atten-tion she was quietly returned to her country home.

been wheedled by his companions into paying ten cents of this sum and was arguing for the return of at least a part of his money, because of the age and helplessness of the woman and the **extreme short time** allowed him by his companions in his relations with her.

Mr. J. J. Sloan, when he was superintendent of the John Worthy School, which is the local juvenile municipal reformatory, reported that one-third of the street boys sent to him were suffering from the loathsome diseases and distempers of the red-light district, nor is this to be wondered at when we consider the fact that sexual commerce may be purchased almost anywhere in South State street and in the West Side alleys for the remarkably low price of ten cents, or even a glass of beer or whiskey, from the gonorrheal, syphilitic denizens thrown out long ago from the better class houses of prostitution to live off of the half-drunken men and boys to be found in swarms along South State, Halsted and South Clark streets.

Almost invariably, the street boy haunting these underworld sections of our city is first led into sexual sin by one of the crippled, half-rotten, yet painted vampires of the streets whose only care or hope is a crust of free lunch and enough whiskey or "dope" to drown for a time at least the last throb of heart and conscience and keep life a little longer in the wretched body, and the boy having purchased for a small fee his own destruction trails out again into the night and on into disease and crime and prison, and finally death.

The average parent of to-day has little idea of the temptations which constantly surround and beset the growing boy. I recall a case in Des Moines, Iowa, where a little degenerate girl of sixteen caused the moral, and in several cases physical, ruin of five young boys, all this happening in an exclusive East Side neighborhood and under the watchful care of honest parents and friends, so what must be the temptation thrown out to the young boys of our city when through block after block of our central districts they must come in contact with those whose only mission is to ruin and debauch.

It should be the direct object, morally and physically, of every father and mother in this city to banish these parasites—these leeches who suck the life blood of our boys—from Chicago's streets.

Listen, father, mother, there are thirty thousand pure, dearly beloved young girls growing up in our midst to-day who within five years must, under the present business system of White Slavery, put aside father, mother, home, friends and honor, and march into Chicago's ghastly flesh market to take the place of the thirty thousand helpless, hopeless, decaying chattels who now daily, behind bolts and bars and steel screens (see note**), satisfy the abomin-

------

**Visit any of the great line of abandoned houses in the red-light district of Custom House Place or Plymouth Court and note the bars and screens and underground steel doors.

able lust of (approximately) two hundred and ten thousand brutal, drunken adulterers.

I believe, as I write, that the final solving of this reeking, hideous question lies in the moral and Christian teaching and protection of the growing girls of our Land. I believe in a rigidly enforced law that keeps girls under legal age and unattended, off the down town streets at nights after a reasonable hour. Harry Balding, the convicted White Slaver, in his confession before Judge Newcomer and State's Attorney Roe, said:

"We would be sent out by resort keepers to work up some girls, for whom we were paid from $10 to $50 dollars each, though the cash bonus was much more. The majority of them were girls we met on the streets. We would go around to the penny arcades and nickel theaters, and when we saw a couple of young girls we would go up and talk with them. I will say for myself—I never took a girl away from her home; the girls I took down there I met in the stores or on the streets."

There is a league of Masonry worldwide that makes it possible for a Mason anywhere, in trouble or distress, to raise his hand toward the heavens with a certain sign, and if there be a brother Mason within reach, that brother, no matter of what nationality, kindred or tongue, is sworn to give him all needed protection. Listen, father, mother, sister; listen, brother!

To-day from beneath Chicago's awful moral sewerage system, which has sucked their hearts and souls under, thirty thousand trembling

hands are held up to High Heaven and to you
for help, hands reeking with the blood on which
some whore monger has fattened, the hands
though of your sisters and of mine. And I believe
that here in Chicago, the greatest market for
White Slaves on the Continent, should be formed
a league that would become world-wide, of earnest, law-abiding men and women whose efforts,
united with those of the proper police, municipal
and Federal authorities, would make it practically impossible for a girl to be sold into or
compelled to lead an immoral life, and through
whose influence such open, publicly-protected
flesh markets as our red-light and levee districts
would be banished forever from Chicago streets.
And I believe with all my heart that this can only
be accomplished by education, by agitation, by
legislation, by the ballot and by the power of
God, directing a great national army of well in-
formed, moral and Christian men and women
against this vast, thoroughly organized, well
administered and heavily financed public horror
of our Republic.

I believe in helping, God knows, with heart
and hand and money every fallen, or as one has
put it, every "knocked down" woman in our
Land whom there is the slightest chance to help
in any way; but I believe, first of all, in using
every known measure to **keep our girls from
falling.**

You and I live beneath the only flag in all the
world that has never known defeat, and the very
basic principle upon which that flag is built is

human liberty and human protection, and so by personal work and co-operation with every other reform and labor organization for the up-lifting of womanhood, by song and by prayer and the Power of the Cross, let us set ourselves to help these helpless ones in our midst until the angels shall take up the story of shame and bitterness and wrong and bear to all the world and to Heaven itself the swift acknowledgment that you are your brother's keeper.

The above picture is from a Flashlight Photograph taken by the author and is a side view of 114 Custom House Place. The demolishing of 116 Custom House Place and several adjacent buildings gave the chance of a life time in securing this and many other photographs. The demolishing of these houses, which up to three years ago were used exclusively for purposes of prostitution, brought to view a perfect network of bars, screens and steel doors (see heavy steel door at right of cut) scarcely dreamed of before as existing outside of our State Penitentiaries.

A dozen Christian Homes and a Municipal Lodging House care for the friendless down-and-out man.   The

Chicago Rescue Mission's Woman's Shelter

cares for the Friendless "down-and-out" Woman.   Our Shelter is not a "Rescue Home" in the ordinary sense of the word, but

A Place where a Clean Bed, Food, Coffee and Clothing may be Obtained by any Homeless Woman

not a subject for Police interference, for One or More nights as she needs; and where she is given Definite Aid to Immediate Employment and assured of shelter until she receives her week's wages.

FIVE THOUSAND AND FORTY NIGHT'S LODGINGS
TOGETHER WITH
OVER SIX THOUSAND MEALS

have been furnished to cold, hungry, Stranded Girls and Women this year by Our Institution.

Seventy per Cent of These Have been Aided to Secure Honest Employment,

but scores have been turned away because we lacked Equipment, Warmth, Funds, etc., to aid them.

Schedule of Work

Year ending August 31st, 1911.

Number of Night's Lodgings Furnished by the Chicago Rescue Mission's Woman Shelter..5,040

Number of Meals 5,200

Special Lodgings............................... 489

Special Meals................................. 677

Calls and Distribution of Fruit at Oak Forest Poor House..................................4,914

Religious Services White Cross Woman's Shelter   26

Jail, Court and Slum Visits................. 1,210

Reform Literature Distributed, pages, about..300,000

Yours and His,

CHICAGO RESCUE MISSION

733-735-737 Washington Blvd.,
NEAR HALSTED

CHICAGO, ILL.

PHONE MONROE 4833

Mrs. Jean T. Zimmermann, M. D.
President Chicago Rescue Mission and Woman's Shelter.
Superintendent Department of Health and Heredity of the Cook County and Chicago W. C. T. U.